T0400578

TOOLS FOR CAREGIVERS

- **F&P LEVEL:** C
- **WORD COUNT:** 37

- **CURRICULUM CONNECTIONS:** animals, colors, habitats, nature, textures

Skills to Teach

- **HIGH-FREQUENCY WORDS:** a, are, has, in, is, it, there, this
- **CONTENT WORDS:** black, bumps, eyes, frog(s), lip, red, spots, stripe, tree, white, yellow
- **PUNCTUATION:** exclamation point, periods
- **WORD STUDY:** digraph *th* (*there*, *this*); long /e/, spelled *ee* (*tree*); long /o/, spelled *ow* (*yellow*); short /o/ (*frog*, *spots*)
- **TEXT TYPE:** information report

Before Reading Activities

- Read the title and give a simple statement of the main idea.
- Have students "walk" through the book and talk about what they see in the pictures.
- Introduce new vocabulary by having students predict the first letter and locate the word in the text.
- Discuss any unfamiliar concepts that are in the text.

After Reading Activities

Talk to the readers about frogs. Explain that there are many kinds. Tree frogs are very good at climbing. Flip back through the book with readers and note the images. What do readers notice about the frogs' feet? How do they think tree frogs' feet help them climb trees?

Tadpole Books are published by Jump!, 5357 Penn Avenue South, Minneapolis, MN 55419, www.jumplibrary.com

Editor: Jenna Gleisner **Designer:** Emma Almgren-Bersie

Photo Credits: kazoka/Shutterstock, cover; Kurit afshen/Shutterstock, 1, 4–5; JasonOndreicka/iStock, 2tl, 6–7; Studio DMM Photography/Shutterstock, 2tr, 8–9; Davemhuntphotography/Dreamstime, 2ml, 10–11; reptiles4all/Shutterstock, 2mr, 14–15; unpict/Shutterstock, 2bl, 12–13; Danita Delimont/Shutterstock, 2br, 3; Shutterstock, 16.

Library of Congress Cataloging-in-Publication Data
Names: Deniston, Natalie, author.
Title: Tree frogs / by Natalie Deniston.
Description: Minneapolis, MN: Jump!, Inc., [2024]
Series: My first animal books | Includes index.
Audience: Ages 3–6
Identifiers: LCCN 2023022284 (print)
LCCN 2023022285 (ebook)
ISBN 9798889965923 (hardcover)
ISBN 9798889965930 (paperback)
ISBN 9798889965947 (ebook)
Subjects: LCSH: Hylidae—Juvenile literature.
Frogs—Juvenile literature.
Classification: LCC QL668.E24 D46 2024 (print)
LCC QL668.E24 (ebook)
DDC 597.87/8—dc23/eng/20230509
LC record available at https://lccn.loc.gov/2023022284
LC ebook record available at https://lccn.loc.gov/2023022285

TREE FROGS

by Natalie Deniston

TABLE OF CONTENTS

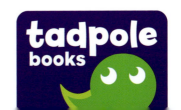

tadpole books

WORDS TO KNOW

bumps

eyes

lip

spots

stripe

tree

TREE FROGS

It is a tree.

There are frogs in it!

bump

This frog has bumps.

eye

This frog has red eyes.

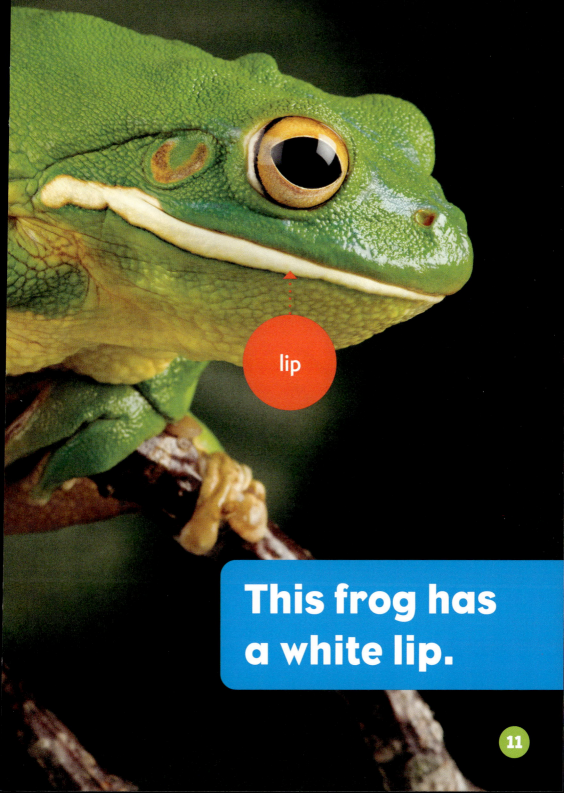

lip

This frog has a white lip.

stripe

This frog has a black stripe.

spot

This frog has yellow spots.

LET'S REVIEW!

All tree frogs can climb trees. Many live in trees. What other animals live in trees?

INDEX